Letts

KS1 Success

Age 5-7

Maths

SATs Revision Guide

Revision Guide

Trevor Dixon

Contents

Number and Place Value

Calculations

Fractions

Measurement

Geometry

Statistics

Mixed Practice Questions

Counting forwards

Being able to count is very important.

Start by **counting forwards** in **ones**: 1 2 3 4 5…

As you become more used to numbers, you can count in different ways.

Count forwards in **twos**:

   2 4 6 8 10… and so on

Count forwards in **threes**:

   1 2 **3** 4 5 **6** 7 8 **9** 10 11 **12** 13 14 **15** 16 17 **18** 19 20 **21**

Count forwards in **fives**:

   1 2 3 4 **5** 6 7 8 9 **10** 11 12 13 14 **15** 16 17 18 19 **20**

Count forwards in **tens**:

   1 2 3 4 5 6 7 8 9 **10** 11 12 13 14 15 16 17 18 19 **20**

Top tip!

When you count forwards (such as in twos), you are **adding** that number each time.

Counting forwards from any number

You can count forwards from any number.

Count forwards in **twos** from 34:

   34 35 **36** 37 **38** 39 **40** 41 **42**

Count forwards in **fives** from 53:

   53 54 55 56 57 **58** 59 60 61 62 **63** 64 65 66 67 **68**

Count forwards in **tens** from 23:

   23 … **33** … **43** … **53** … **63** … **73** … **83** … **93**

Keyword

Counting forwards ➤ Counting numbers in order, in a group (such as ones, twos, fives), so that the numbers get larger

Counting back

You can also **count back**.

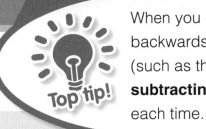

> **Top tip!** When you count backwards in a number (such as threes), you are **subtracting** that number each time.

Count back in **twos**:
  48 47 **46** 45 **44** 43 **42** 41 **40** 39 **38** 37 **36** 35 **34** 33 **32** 31 **30** 29

Count back in **threes**:
  70 69 68 **67** 66 65 **64** 63 62 **61** 60 59 **58** 57 56 **55** 54 53 **52** 51

Counting back from any number

You can count back from any number.

> **Parent tip!** Help your child find patterns in the numbers when they are counting.

Count back in **twos** from 111:
  111 110 **109** 108 **107** 106 **105** 104 **103** 102 **101**

Count back in **threes** from 161:
  161 160 159 **158** 157 156 **155** 154 153 **152** 151 150 **149** 148 147 **146** 145 144 **143**

Count back in **fives** from 267:
  267 266 265 264 263 **262** 261 260 259 258 **257** 256 255 254 253 **252** 251

Count back in **tens** from 342:
  342 … **332** … **322** … **312** … **302** … **292** … **282**

Keyword

Counting back ➤ Counting numbers in reverse order, in a group (such as ones, twos, fives), so that the numbers get smaller

Have a go!

➤ Count forwards in twos by looking at house numbers on one side of a road.

➤ Count forwards in threes when you are walking up stairs.

Test yourself

1 For each question, write the next four numbers.

a. Count back in twos from 51.

b. Count forwards in threes from 57.

c. Count back in fives from 61.

d. Count forwards in tens from 41.

e. Count back in threes from 84.

Place value

Number and Place Value

What is place value?

Every **digit** in a number has a **place value**.

A digit on its own means the number is in units.

5 on its own means five units: ★ ★ ★ ★ ★

If a number has two digits, each digit has a value depending on where it is in the number.

25 means two groups of ten and one group of five units, or 20 + 5.

20: ★ ★ ★ ★ ★ ★ ★ ★ ★ ★
★ ★ ★ ★ ★ ★ ★ ★ ★ ★

+ 5: ★ ★ ★ ★ ★

Finding the value of numbers

You need to know the place value of each digit in a two-digit number.

62	=	**6** tens and **2** units
46	=	**4** tens and **6** units
85	=	**8** tens and **5** units
39	=	**3** tens and **9** units

Keywords

Digit ➤ A number from 0–9 that can be used to make other numbers

Place value ➤ What a digit is worth. This depends on its position in a number

 **Top tip!**

If you are unsure about the place value of a digit, put the number under tens and units columns.

Tens   Units
4   3
4 tens + 3 units = 43

 Listen up 2

Using an abacus

An **abacus** shows the place values of numbers.

The abacuses below show the place values for 27, 43, 45 and 61.

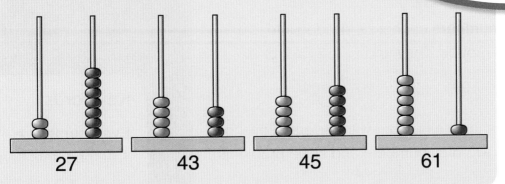

27   43   45   61

Parent tip! If you have an abacus, make up some problems. Otherwise, draw an abacus on paper and add the beads by hand.

Keyword

Abacus ➤ A tool for displaying numbers

Using place value to help you add and subtract

If you know the place value of each digit in a number, it will help you when you add and subtract.

Top tip! Always think about place value when you add or subtract.

Example questions:

$45 + 30 = ?$

Add 3 tens

```
   4 5
+  3 0
-----
   7 5
```

$45 - 30 = ?$

Take 3 tens away

```
   4 5
-  3 0
-----
   1 5
```

Have a go! Look for two-digit numbers, for example on houses or at the supermarket.

➤ Which is the tens digit and which is the units digit?

Test yourself

❶ What are the missing numbers?

a. $67 = \_\_ + 7$

b. $\_\_ = 50 + 9$

c. $28 = 20 + \_\_$

❷ Work out:

a. $63 + 20 = \_\_$

b. $87 - 5 = \_\_$

c. $68 - 40 = \_\_$

Even and odd numbers

Even numbers can be divided into two equal groups. They end in 0, 2, 4, 6 or 8.

| 40 | 52 | 24 | 76 | 38 |

Odd numbers cannot be divided into two equal groups. They end in 1, 3, 5, 7 or 9.

| 21 | 93 | 25 | 87 | 69 |

You can use a number with several digits to make two-digit numbers and solve problems.

Here are three digit cards.

- The smallest, odd, two-digit number you can make from the cards is 29.
- The smallest, even, two-digit number you can make from the cards is 24.
- The largest, even, two-digit number you can make from the cards is 94.

Keywords

Even number ➤ A number that can be divided exactly by 2

Odd number ➤ A number that cannot be divided exactly by 2

Numbers and shapes

Sometimes shapes are used to represent numbers.

stands for 10   and   **stands for 1**

So, 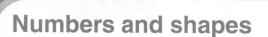 **stands for 24**

Example question: Which numbers do these shapes stand for?

1 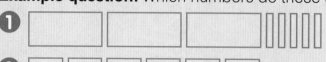 **stands for 35**

2  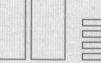 **stands for 68**

Number lines

A **number line** shows numbers in order.

Talk about the missing values on weighing scales.

Parent tip!

The arrow is pointing to a number just past 15. It is pointing to 16.

Some number lines miss out numbers. They might just show tens, fives or twos.

Keyword

Number line
➤ Shows the position of a number. The numbers can be listed in different ways, for example ones, twos, fives, tens, and so on

Example question:
For each number line, write the number the arrow points to.

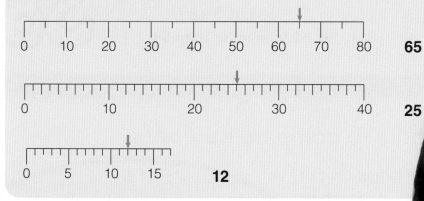

65

25

12

Listen up

3

Look at page numbers in the book you are reading, at the numbers on supermarket aisles and the numbers on the front of buses.

➤ What number comes next?

➤ What number came before?

Have a go!

Test yourself

1 Here is a set of numbers:

8   3   6   1   4

Use these numbers to make:

a. the largest, odd, two-digit number

b. the largest, even, two-digit number with 6 tens.

2 What number does the arrow point to?

Comparing numbers

It is useful to compare numbers and work out when one number is bigger or smaller than another. When you compare numbers, think about place value.

Parent tip! When comparing numbers, always look at the highest-value digit first.

Example question 1: Which is bigger: 62 or 37?

62 is made of 6 tens and 2 units   37 is made of 3 tens and 7 units
6 tens is more than 3 tens. The units are not as important.
So, 62 is bigger than 37.

Example question 2: Which is smaller: 58 or 53?

Both numbers have 5 tens, so you need to look at the units.
58 has 8 units   53 has 3 units
3 units is less than 8 units. **So, 53 is smaller than 58.**

Using symbols to compare numbers

Instead of writing 'is bigger than' or 'is less than', you can use **symbols**.
- = means is the same as
- < means is smaller than
- > means is bigger than

Top tip! To help remember < and >, think of a crocodile eating the larger numbers. The arrow always points to the smaller number.

Using the example above, 62 'is bigger than' 37 can be written as 62 > 37.

45	<	61	means that 45 'is smaller than' 61
89	>	29	means that 89 'is bigger than' 29
93	>	73	means that 93 'is bigger than' 73
10	<	71	means that 10 'is smaller than' 71
12	=	12	means that 12 'is equal to' 12

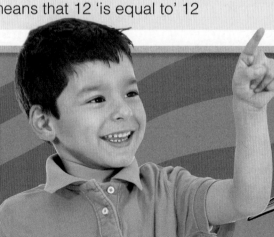

Keyword

Symbols ➤ Signs that are used instead of words

Number and Place Value

Ordering numbers

You can arrange numbers in order.

For example, these numbers are in order, starting with the largest number.

We can use place value to find the largest and smallest numbers.

Example question: Put these numbers in order, starting with the smallest.

75   29   53   60   71

1 Find the tens digit with the smallest value first; in this case, **2**9, **5**3, **6**0.

2 There are two numbers with 7 tens, so now use the units digit.
In this case, 7**1** is smaller than 7**5**.

So, starting with the smallest number, the numbers in order are **29, 53, 60, 71, 75**.

When you are writing numbers over twenty, use a hyphen.

Numbers written as words

This table shows examples of two-digit numbers written as words.

Number	Word
67	sixty-seven
73	seventy-three
85	eighty-five
16	sixteen
49	forty-nine

Make a set of cards using the numbers 0 to 9.

➤ **Make two two-digit numbers. Compare the numbers and work out which number is bigger.**

➤ **Repeat this five times.**

➤ **Then have five turns at identifying the smaller number.**

1 Insert < or > in the circles to compare these numbers.

a. 83 ◯ 81   b. 91 ◯ 57

c. 17 ◯ 32   d. 77 ◯ 68

2 Put these numbers in order, starting with the largest number.

56   81   30   27   24

3 Write seventy-two as a number.

This mind map will help you remember all the main points from this topic. Have a go at drawing your own mind map.

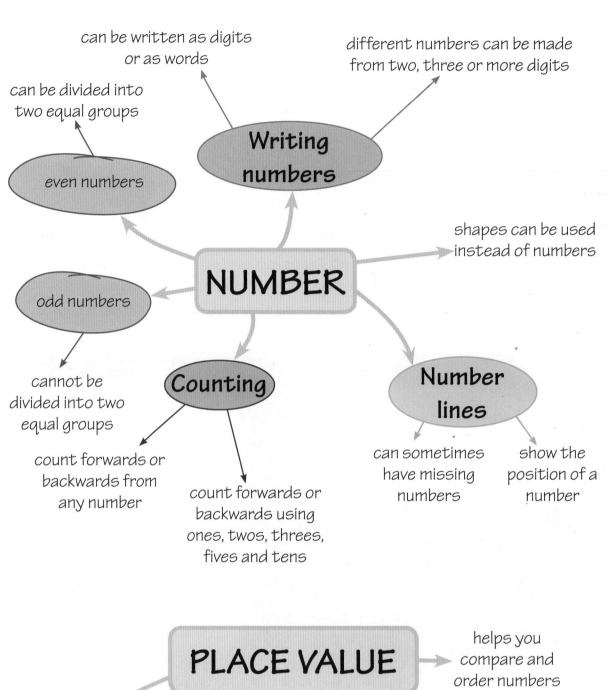

can be written as digits or as words

different numbers can be made from two, three or more digits

can be divided into two equal groups

Writing numbers

even numbers

shapes can be used instead of numbers

NUMBER

odd numbers

cannot be divided into two equal groups

Counting

Number lines

count forwards or backwards from any number

count forwards or backwards using ones, twos, threes, fives and tens

can sometimes have missing numbers

show the position of a number

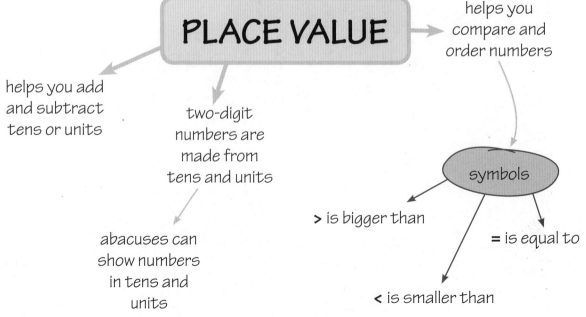

PLACE VALUE

helps you compare and order numbers

helps you add and subtract tens or units

two-digit numbers are made from tens and units

symbols

abacuses can show numbers in tens and units

> is bigger than

= is equal to

< is smaller than

1 What are the next five numbers in each sequence?

    a. 35 38 41 44 ....   **(1 mark)**

    b. 67 62 57 52 ....   **(1 mark)**

    c. 84 86 88 90 ....   **(1 mark)**

    d. 5 15 25 35 ....   **(1 mark)**

2 Fill in the spaces.

    a. 68 = ... tens and .... units   **(1 mark)**

    b. .... = 7 tens and 8 units   **(1 mark)**

    c. 91 = ... tens and .... unit   **(1 mark)**

    d. ...... 4 = 3 tens and .... units   **(1 mark)**

3 What number does each abacus show?   **(2 marks)**

    a.   **b.**

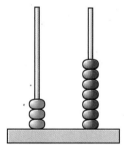   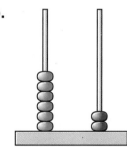

    ....

4 Here are three digit cards.   **(4 marks)**

    a. Use them to make six different **two-digit** numbers.

    ....

    b. Now put your numbers in order, starting with the lowest.

    ....

5 Write **<** or **>** in each circle to compare these numbers.   **(2 marks)**

    a. 56 ◯ 28   **b.** 79 ◯ 83

6 Write this number in words.   59: ....   **(1 mark)**

7 Write this as a number.   forty-five: ....   **(1 mark)**

Adding

+ means 'add' **= means 'equals'** or **'is the same as'**
Add numbers together by counting forwards.
Start by **adding** one-digit numbers together.
It does not matter in which order you add numbers.

When you add two-digit numbers, you can use **partitioning**.

Top tip! Knowing simple sums like 4 + 3 = 7 will help you do harder sums like 34 + 3 = 37 and 84 + 3 = 87.

Example question: 64 + 5 = ?

64 = 60 + 4
So adding 64 + 5 is the same as adding 60 + 4 + 5   4 + 5 = 9
64 + 5 = **69**

Adding aids

Write down harder sums.
Try to remember **adding words**.
You can use a number line to count forwards.

Example question: 54 + 38 = ?

```
   +30    +6    +2
54      84    90    92
```

So, 54 + 38 = **92**

You can also use partitioning.

Example question: 54 + 38 = ?

```
  5 4 = 5 0  +   4
+ 3 8   3 0  +   8
        8 0  +  12
        8 0  +  10 + 2 = 92
```

Keywords

Adding ➤ Combining two or more numbers to give a total or a sum
Partitioning ➤ Splitting numbers using place value
Adding words ➤ Words that show you may have to add, such as 'altogether', 'extra', 'more', 'plus', 'sum' and 'total'

Subtracting

– means 'subtract'   **= means 'equals' or 'is the same as'**

Subtract numbers by counting back. It does matter in which order you subtract numbers.

> 8 – 3 = 5 but 3 – 8 does not equal 5

Start by **subtracting** one-digit numbers. Learning basic subtraction facts will help with subtraction sums.

 Look for patterns in numbers.

Subtracting SOS

Write down harder sums. Use subtraction methods to help you. Try to remember **subtracting words**.

You can use a number line to count back.

> **Example question:** 53 – 24 = ?
>
> $$-1 \quad -3 \quad -20$$
> 29   30   33   53
>
> So, 53 – 24 = **29**

You can also use partitioning.

> **Example question:** 53 – 24 = ?
>
> Here, you 'borrow' ten from 50 and add to the 3.
>
> $$\begin{array}{rcrcr} & & 4\,0 & & 13 \\ 5\,3 & = & 5\,0 & + & 3 \\ -\,2\,4 & & 2\,0 & + & 4 \\ \hline & & 2\,0 & + & 9 = \mathbf{29} \end{array}$$

Keywords

Subtracting ➤ Taking one number from another to leave a difference

Subtracting words ➤ Words that show you may have to subtract, such as 'difference', 'fewer', 'left', 'less than', 'minus', 'reduce' and 'take away'

Listen up 5

 **Have a go!** When you go shopping, add the prices of some of the things you buy. Try to work out the change you will get.

 **Test yourself**

Work out:

1 a. 17 + 1 =   b. 43 + 2 =

    c. 7 + 6 + 8 =   d. 72 + 34 =

2 a. 20 – 1 =   b. 28 – 26 =

    c. 78 – 69 =   d. 91 – 36 =

Multiplying

When you are **multiplying**, you are counting or adding in steps of the same number.

> $2 + 2 + 2 + 2 + 2 = 10$
> Here, we add five twos to make 10.
> Another way to write this is $2 \times 5 = 10$.

It does not matter in which order you multiply numbers. Try to remember **multiplication words**.

$4 \times 2 = 8$ is the same as $2 \times 4 = 8$

Top tip!

When you learn the multiplication facts, look for patterns in the numbers. Practise, practise, practise!

We can show multiplication facts as arrays.

Below is an array for 5×2. This array can be turned around to 2×5.

5×2 2×5

This array also shows $5 + 5 = 10$
Writing this as five times two is $5 \times 2 = 10$

These sums are the same:
$2 + 2 + 2 + 2 + 2 = 2 \times 5 = 10$
$5 + 5 = 5 \times 2 = 10$

Keywords

Multiplying ➤ Counting or adding in steps of the same number

Multiplication words ➤ Words that show you may have to multiply, such as 'by', 'double', 'lots', 'times' and 'twice'

Dividing

When you are **dividing** a number, you are splitting it into equal parts.

$$15 \div 5 = ?$$

There are **3** groups of 5.

Also think of dividing as sharing the number equally.

$15 \div 5 = ?$

15 shared between 5, which is **3**.

It does matter in which order you divide numbers. Try to remember **division words**.

Parent tip! Encourage your child to learn division facts by using the opposite of multiplication facts.

Division facts

If you know a multiplication fact, you should be able to work out the division fact.

If you know that	$4 \times 5 = 20$
you can work out that	$20 \div 5 = 4$

4 times 5 is 20, so splitting 20 into five groups is 4.

You also know that	$5 \times 4 = 20$
so, you can work out that	$20 \div 4 = 5$

Keywords

Dividing ➤ To split or share a number equally

Division words ➤ Words that show you may have to divide, such as 'each', 'every', 'half', 'quarter', 'share', 'split' and 'third'

Have a go! Try sharing objects, such as toys, beads or counters, into equal groups.

➤ Write down your calculation, for example: $6 \div 2 = 3$

➤ Think about what you would do if you had any objects left over.

Test yourself

Work out:

1 a. $3 \times 5 =$ ___   b. $4 \times 2 =$ ___

     c. $7 \times 10 =$ ___   d. $7 \times 5 =$ ___

2 a. $12 \div 2 =$ ___   b. $40 \div 5 =$ ___

     c. $60 \div 10 =$ ___   d. $45 \div 5 =$ ___

3 Write the missing signs:

     a. $10 \bigcirc 5 = 50$

     b. $50 \bigcirc 10 = 5$

Checking answers

You can use subtraction to check addition sums.

> $26 + 35 = \textbf{61}$
> To check the answer is correct, you can work out:
> $\quad \textbf{61} - 35 = 26$
> or
> $\quad \textbf{61} - 26 = 35$

You can also use addition to check subtraction questions.

> $72 - 48 = \textbf{24}$
> To check the answer is correct, you can work out:
> $\quad \textbf{24} + 48 = 72$

Missing number problems

You might be asked to find a missing number in a question.
Think carefully about the order in which to write the two numbers.
Do you need to add or subtract them?

> **Example question:** Find the missing numbers:
>
> $\quad 45 + \underline{} = 87 \qquad 73 - \underline{} = 27 \qquad \underline{} \times 5 = 35 \qquad 20 \div \underline{} = 10$
>
> **Answers:**
>
> $\quad 87 - 45 = \textbf{42} \qquad 73 - 27 = \textbf{46} \qquad 35 \div 5 = \textbf{7} \qquad 20 \div 10 = \textbf{2}$
>
> **Now check your answers.**
>
> $\quad 45 + \textbf{42} = 87 \qquad 73 - \textbf{46} = 27 \qquad \textbf{7} \times 5 = 35 \qquad 20 \div \textbf{2} = 10$

Listen up
7

Parent tip!

Encourage your child to check their answers using another kind of calculation, e.g. subtraction for addition sums.

Different ways of showing questions

Here are some different ways of showing multiplication and division questions.

$10 + 10 + 10 + 10 + 10$　　　=　　10×5　=　50

=　　2×10　=　20

Shareen and Sam have 12 sweets.

They share the sweets.

How many do they each get?　　　　$12 \div 2$　=　6

What if they have 14 sweets?

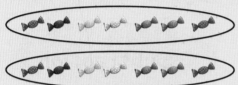

$14 \div 2$　=　7

Nia has six 10p coins.

How much money does she have?　　　10×6　=　60p

Remember:

- All even numbers can be divided by 2.
- Numbers ending in 5 or 0 can be divided by 5.
- Numbers ending in 0 can be divided by 10.

Parent tip!

Playing games and doing puzzles are a good way to learn. Try this puzzle: Pick four one-digit numbers. How many even numbers can you make?

Have a go!

Make sure you know which numbers are even and which are odd.

➤ Check to see which unit digits make a number odd and which make a number even.

➤ When you are in the supermarket, have a look at the numbers on the aisles. Are they even or odd?

Test yourself

① a. $56 + \_\_ = 83$

b. $70 - \_\_ = 62$

c. $4 + \_\_ + 3 = 15$

② Sort these numbers into odd numbers and even numbers.

15　　28　　93　　36

70　　81　　52

③ Write a calculation for these drawings:

a. ★★★★　　b. ★★★★★★
★★★★☆　　　★★★★★★
★★★★

This mind map will help you remember all the main points from this topic. Have a go at drawing your own mind map.

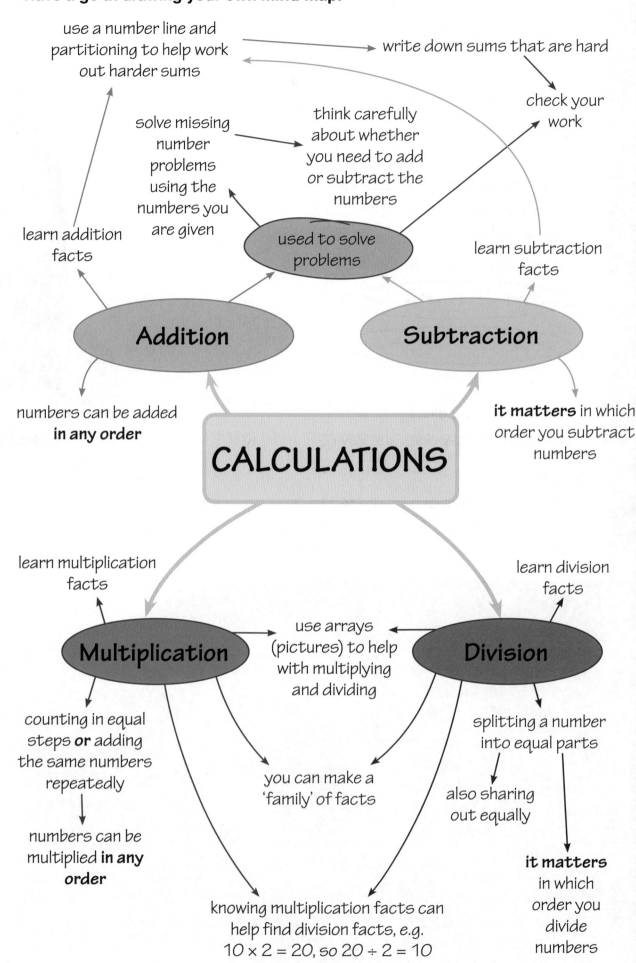

use a number line and partitioning to help work out harder sums

write down sums that are hard

check your work

solve missing number problems using the numbers you are given

think carefully about whether you need to add or subtract the numbers

used to solve problems

learn addition facts

learn subtraction facts

Addition

Subtraction

numbers can be added **in any order**

it matters in which order you subtract numbers

CALCULATIONS

learn multiplication facts

learn division facts

Multiplication

use arrays (pictures) to help with multiplying and dividing

Division

counting in equal steps **or** adding the same numbers repeatedly

you can make a 'family' of facts

splitting a number into equal parts

also sharing out equally

numbers can be multiplied **in any order**

knowing multiplication facts can help find division facts, e.g.
$10 \times 2 = 20$, so $20 \div 2 = 10$

it matters in which order you divide numbers

1 Write the answers to these facts. **(4 marks)**

    a. $5 + 6 = \ldots$ **b.** $7 - 4 = \ldots$ **c.** $80 \div 10 = \ldots$ **d.** $30 \div 5 = \ldots$

2 Add these numbers. **(4 marks)**

    a. $6 + 3 + 4 = \ldots$ **b.** $7 + 7 + 5 = \ldots$ **c.** $4 + 9 + 5 = \ldots$ **d.** $8 + 5 + 4 = \ldots$

3 Work out: **(3 marks)**

    a. $67 + 7 = \ldots$ **b.** $83 - 5 = \ldots$ **c.** $70 - 16 = \ldots$

4 Find the missing numbers. **(3 marks)**

    a. $34 + \ldots = 43$ **b.** $5 \times \ldots = 50$ **c.** $\ldots \div 2 = 5$

5 Here is a list of numbers. **(2 marks)**
Circle the odd numbers.

       34   56   7   29   74   19   90

6 Write the missing sign ($\times$ or $\div$).

    a. $4 \bigcirc 5 = 20$ **b.** $40 \bigcirc 5 = 8$ **(2 marks)**

7 Write both calculations as multiplications. Then complete the answers.

    a. $6 + 6 + 6 + 6 + 6 = \ldots\ldots\ldots\ldots\ldots\ldots\ldots\ldots\ldots\ldots\ldots$ **(2 marks)**

    $\ldots\ldots\ldots\ldots\ldots\ldots\ldots\ldots\ldots\ldots\ldots\ldots\ldots\ldots\ldots\ldots\ldots\ldots\ldots\ldots$

    b. $9 + 9 = \ldots\ldots\ldots\ldots\ldots\ldots\ldots\ldots\ldots\ldots\ldots\ldots\ldots\ldots\ldots\ldots$ **(2 marks)**

    $\ldots\ldots\ldots\ldots\ldots\ldots\ldots\ldots\ldots\ldots\ldots\ldots\ldots\ldots\ldots\ldots\ldots\ldots\ldots\ldots$

8 Solve these problems.

    a. Chetna had 45 cards. She got another 25 cards.
        How many cards did Chetna have altogether?   **(2 marks)**

    $\ldots\ldots\ldots\ldots\ldots\ldots\ldots\ldots\ldots\ldots\ldots\ldots\ldots\ldots\ldots\ldots\ldots\ldots\ldots\ldots\ldots\ldots\ldots\ldots$

    b. Ali has a book with 70 pages. He has read 28 pages.
        How many pages does he have left to read?   **(2 marks)**

    $\ldots\ldots\ldots\ldots\ldots\ldots\ldots\ldots\ldots\ldots\ldots\ldots\ldots\ldots\ldots\ldots\ldots\ldots\ldots\ldots\ldots\ldots\ldots\ldots$

    c. Mia has 20 seeds. She has 5 pots and puts the same
        number of seeds into each pot.
        How many seeds does Mia put into each pot?   **(2 marks)**

    $\ldots\ldots\ldots\ldots\ldots\ldots\ldots\ldots\ldots\ldots\ldots\ldots\ldots\ldots\ldots\ldots\ldots\ldots\ldots\ldots\ldots\ldots\ldots\ldots$

Fractions

A **fraction** is a part of a whole number.

The whole may be an object, a shape, or a quantity like a weight or money.

A fraction is made up of **two parts** but it is **one number**.

$\frac{3}{4}$

The top number (**numerator**) tells you how many parts you have.

You have 3 of the parts.

The bottom number (**denominator**) tells you how many parts the whole is divided into.

There are 4 parts in the whole.

Keywords

Fraction ➤ A number that shows the part or parts of one whole

Numerator ➤ The top number in a fraction that shows the number of parts you have

Denominator ➤ The bottom number in a fraction that shows the number of parts in the whole

 Parent tip! Help your child to understand the numerator and denominator by using real-life examples such as slices of pizza.

Fraction names

Fraction	Fraction name	What they look like
$\frac{1}{2}$	one half	
$\frac{1}{3}$	one third	
$\frac{1}{4}$	one quarter	
$\frac{2}{4}$	two quarters	

Listen up 8

Solving fraction problems

To work out what fraction of a shape is shaded:

- find out how many parts are in the shape (this is the bottom number of the fraction)
- see how many parts are shaded (this is the top number of the fraction).

Example question:

What fraction of this shape is shaded?

There are 4 parts in the shape.
So the shape is in quarters and the bottom number of the fraction is 4.
1 part of the shape is shaded. So the top number of the fraction is 1.
$\frac{1}{4}$ of the shape is shaded.

Fractions and equal parts

When one whole shape is split into **equal** parts, each part is the same. It does not matter which part of the shape is shaded.

These squares are divided into 4 equal parts. Each red shaded part of this shape is $\frac{1}{4}$.

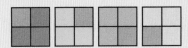

Remember, the same fractions of a shape must be the same size.

Only the ticked shape shows $\frac{1}{4}$ even though all the shapes have four parts with one part shaded purple.

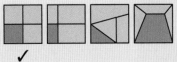

There are many different-sized shapes. Their fractions will have different shapes and sizes too.

Find or draw some shapes and draw lines to divide them into halves or quarters.

Remember to split the shape into equal parts. Equal fractions in a shape should be the same size.

❶ **What fraction is shaded?**

a.   b.

❷ **Write the letter of the shape that has $\frac{1}{3}$ shaded.**

A   B

C   D

Equivalent fractions

Some fractions look different but have the same value.

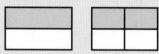

Look at these two shapes. They are the same size.

One shape has $\frac{1}{2}$ shaded and the other shape has $\frac{2}{4}$ shaded.
Both shapes have the same amount of shading.
$\frac{1}{2}$ and $\frac{2}{4}$ are the same.
They are **equivalent** fractions.

Fraction wall

A fraction wall helps you compare fractions.
You can see which fractions are bigger, which
are smaller and which are the same (equivalent).

One whole = 1			
$\frac{1}{2}$		$\frac{1}{2}$	
$\frac{1}{3}$	$\frac{1}{3}$		$\frac{1}{3}$
$\frac{1}{4}$	$\frac{1}{4}$	$\frac{1}{4}$	$\frac{1}{4}$

Top tip! The bigger the digit is for the bottom number of a fraction, the smaller the fraction.

Finding a fraction of a number

To **find a fraction of a number**, divide the number by the bottom number of the fraction. Then multiply that number by the top number of the fraction. The answer will be the same if you use equivalent fractions.

Example questions:

What is $\frac{1}{2}$ of 20?

$20 \div 2 = 10$

$10 \times 1 = 10$

$\frac{1}{2}$ of 20 = **10**

What is $\frac{2}{4}$ of 20?

$20 \div 4 = 5$

$5 \times 2 = 10$

$\frac{2}{4}$ of 20 = **10**

Finding fractions of shape and quantity

To **find a fraction of a shape**:
- split the shape into equal parts
- shade the correct part.

When you find a fraction of a shape, quantity or number, all the parts or fractions need to be the same size or equal.

Top tip!

Example question: Shade $\frac{1}{3}$ of this shape.

First, divide the shape into three equal parts.

Then shade one part.

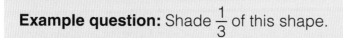

To **find a fraction of a quantity**:
- count the whole quantity
- divide that number by the bottom number of the fraction.

Example question: Find $\frac{1}{4}$ of these counters.

First, count the number of counters – this is the whole group.

There are 8.

Divide 8 by 4 to split the whole group into 4 equal groups.

You have divided by 4.

$8 \div 4 = 2$ 2 is $\frac{1}{4}$ of 8

Have a go!

Fold an oblong-shaped piece of paper exactly in half. This makes two halves.

➤ What happens when you fold the paper in half again?

➤ What is the fraction you make by folding paper exactly in half twice?

➤ How many different ways can you fold a piece of paper in half twice?

➤ Is it easier if the paper is in a square shape?

Test yourself

❶ Write the missing number.

$$\frac{\square}{4} = \frac{1}{2}$$

❷ Work out:

a. $\frac{1}{2}$ of 6   b. $\frac{1}{3}$ of 6

c. $\frac{1}{4}$ of 20

❸ Work out:

a. $\frac{3}{4}$ of 8   b. $\frac{3}{4}$ of 12

c. $\frac{3}{4}$ of 20

This mind map will help you remember all the main points from this topic. Have a go at drawing your own mind map.

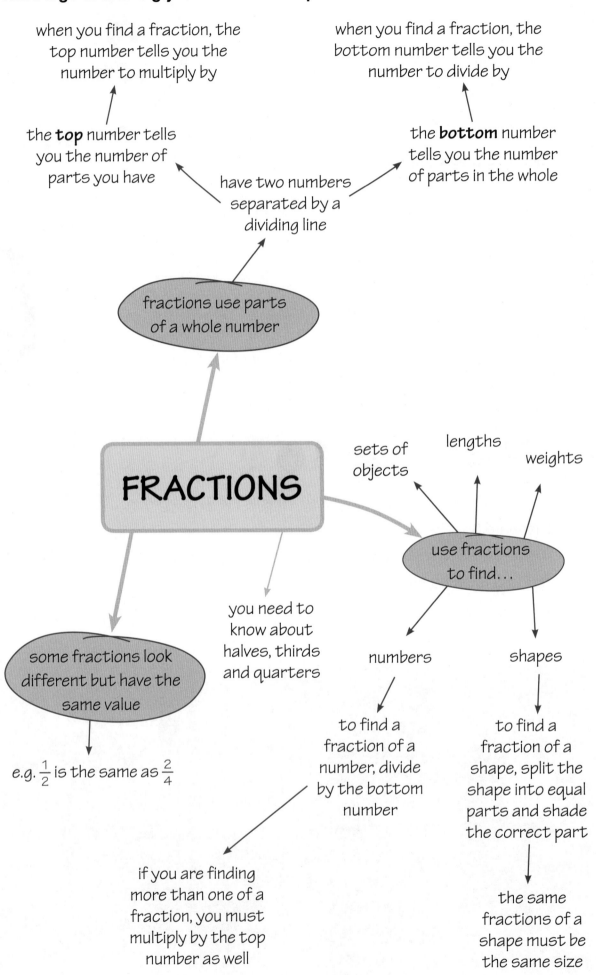

when you find a fraction, the top number tells you the number to multiply by

when you find a fraction, the bottom number tells you the number to divide by

the **top** number tells you the number of parts you have

the **bottom** number tells you the number of parts in the whole

have two numbers separated by a dividing line

fractions use parts of a whole number

FRACTIONS

sets of objects

lengths

weights

use fractions to find...

you need to know about halves, thirds and quarters

numbers

shapes

some fractions look different but have the same value

e.g. $\frac{1}{2}$ is the same as $\frac{2}{4}$

to find a fraction of a number, divide by the bottom number

to find a fraction of a shape, split the shape into equal parts and shade the correct part

if you are finding more than one of a fraction, you must multiply by the top number as well

the same fractions of a shape must be the same size

1 What fraction is shaded in these shapes?

a.  **(1 mark)**   **b.** **(1 mark)**

....

c. **(1 mark)**   **d.** **(1 mark)**

....

2 **a.** Shade $\frac{1}{3}$ of this shape. **(1 mark)**   **b.** Shade $\frac{3}{4}$ of this shape. **(1 mark)**

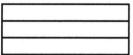 

3 Find: **(4 marks)**

   a. $\frac{1}{4}$ of 12   **b.** $\frac{1}{3}$ of 15   **c.** $\frac{3}{4}$ of 16   **d.** $\frac{1}{2}$ of £40

   ....

4 What fraction of these counters is shaded? **(1 mark)**

....

5 Solve these problems.

   a. Tom has 20 cards. He gives one half of the cards to his friend. **(1 mark)**
      How many cards does Tom give to his friend?

   ....

   b. Polly has 12 teddy bears. One quarter of them are white. **(1 mark)**
      How many teddy bears are white?

   ....

6 Here are four shapes. **(2 marks)**

     A   **B**   **C**   **D**

Write the letters of the two shapes that have the same fraction shaded.

....

Units of measurement

We use **metric units** for measuring.
Use the right unit for what you are measuring.

Length/Height	Weight/Mass	Capacity	Temperature
centimetres metres	grams kilograms	millilitres litres	degrees Celsius

Abbreviations

Here is how to shorten the unit names.

- centimetres   cm
- metres   m
- grams   g
- kilograms   kg
- millilitres   ml
- litres   l
- degrees Celsius   °C

Keyword

Metric units ➤ Measures based on groups of ten

Measuring equipment

Use the correct equipment to measure accurately.

- length/height   ruler, tape measure
- weight/mass   scales, balance
- capacity   measuring jug
- temperature   thermometer

Listen up 10

Measuring length

Use a ruler or a tape measure to measure length.

Top tip!

Look carefully at the numbers on a ruler or tape measure. Think about what the marks in between them mean.

Example question: How long is this pencil?

0 1 2 3 4 5 6 7 8 9 10 11 12 13 14 15 16 17 18 19 20 21 22 23 24 cm

What to do:
1. Line up one end of the pencil with the 0 cm mark.
2. Use the other end of the pencil to read the length on the scale.
3. The tip of the pencil is at the 19 mark, so the pencil is **19 cm long**.

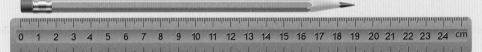

Parent tip!

Give your child practical experience of measuring lengths, weights, capacity and temperature. For instance, ask your child to weigh ingredients or measure the length of a material.

Measuring capacity

Use a measuring jug to measure capacity.

1 Make sure the jug is on a level surface.
2 Read the level of the liquid on the scale.
3 Work out what the marks mean in between the numbers.

Example question:

How much orange squash is in the jug?

What to do:

1 Make sure the jug is on a level surface.
2 Read the level of the orange squash on the scale.
3 The level is half way between 3 and 4 litres, so the level is $3\frac{1}{2}$ litres.

Measuring weight or mass

Use scales or a balance to measure weight or mass.

1 Look where the pointer is on the scales or balance.
2 Work out what the marks mean in between the numbers.

Example question:

What is the weight of the parcel on the scales?

What to do:

1 Look where the pointer is on the scales.
2 The pointer is half way between 400 g and 500 g, so the weight is 450 g.

Have a go!

Try and find the answers to these questions:

➤ How long and wide (in centimetres) is the book you are reading?
➤ How much water can you put in a mug?
➤ How heavy is an apple?
➤ What is the temperature of a cold drink?

Test yourself

1 What weight is shown by the arrow on this scale?

```
0
50 g  ←
100 g
```

2 What is the length of this line?

Look again at the section on *Number and Place Value* on pages 4–11 to remind yourself how to compare numbers and record answers.

Parent tip!

Whenever you can, compare lengths, heights, weights and capacities. Encourage accurate vocabulary.

Estimating and comparing length and height

Before you measure something exactly, try to estimate how long it is in real life.

Example question: Put these objects in order of length, shortest first:

car   bike   train   bus

The answer is: **bike, car, bus, train**

Estimating and comparing weight or mass

When you pick up objects, try to estimate how heavy they are so you can compare them with other objects.

Example question: Put these objects in order of weight, heaviest first:

pumpkin   apple   grape   melon

The answer is: **pumpkin, melon, apple, grape**

Estimating and comparing capacity

Try to estimate how much containers hold in real life.

Example question: Put these objects in order of capacity, smallest first:

bath   milk bottle   drinks can   cup

The answer is: **cup, drinks can, milk bottle, bath**

Measurement symbols

Use these symbols: = is the same as   < is smaller than   > is bigger than

Comparing weights

Remember, 1000 g = 1 kg
Use your place value skills to compare weights that have the same units. You might be asked to compare the weights of objects.

Example question: Compare the weights of a bag of flour and a bag of apples.

1000 g   750 g

1000 g is heavier than 750 g, so
1000 g > 750 g

Comparing lengths

Remember, 100 cm = 1 m
When you compare lengths that have the same units, use your place value skills. You might be asked to compare the lengths of objects.

Example question: Compare the lengths of the car and the bus.

4 m   9 m

4 m is shorter than 9 m, so **4 m < 9 m**

Top tip! Some lengths are **twice** the length of another. For example, 12 m is twice the length of 6 m.

Some lengths are **half** the length of another. For example, 6 m is half the length of 12 m.

Comparing capacities

Remember, 1000 ml = 1 litre
When you compare capacities that have the same units, use your place value skills.

Example question: Compare the capacities of these two jugs.

A 4-litre jug holds more than a 2-litre jug, so **4 litres > 2 litres**.

4 litres

2 litres

Have a go!

➤ Compare the weights of objects on your kitchen scales.

➤ Compare the lengths of different objects. If you do not have a ruler or tape measure, use a piece of string.

➤ Fill different containers with water and then use a measuring jug to see which holds the most.

Test yourself

1 Write < or > in the circles.

a. 6 m ◯ 10 m

b. 17 kg ◯ 11 kg

c. 75 cm ◯ 80 cm

2 Tick the statement that is true.

a. 60 ml is half of 30 ml ▢

b. 100 cm is twice 50 cm ▢

Money

In the UK, there are two symbols for money:

- £ **pounds**
- p **pence** or **pennies**

£1 = 100p

Use £ or p, but not both together.

> You could have:
> £1.25 or 125p, **not** £1.25p

If you write money with the point, you must always have two numbers after it.

> £2 = £2.00 **not** £2.0

Keywords

Pounds ➤ A unit of money. 100 pence make £1. £1 is the same as 100 pennies

Pence/pennies ➤ A unit of money. 100 pennies make £1

Coins and notes

There are different coins.
Some coins are in pence.

Some coins are in pounds.

There are also different notes.

Making amounts with coins

When you go shopping you use different coins.

> **Example question:** An apple costs 45p. Which coins could you use to buy it?
>
> - Count out and add up the coins needed to reach 45p.
> - Remember, you can only use coins that are used in real life.
>
> There are lots of possible answers. Here is one:
>
>   20p + 10p + 10p + 5p
>
> You might be able to think of others, including forty-five 1p coins!

Adding up coins

To find the total of a set of coins, add the amounts of all the coins.

Example question: Find the total of these coins.

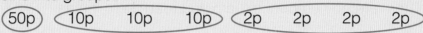

First, sort the coins into groups.

(50p) (10p   10p   10p) (2p   2p   2p   2p)

Then add them up.

one 50p coin		**three 10p coins**		**four 2p coins**	
50p	+	30p	+	8p	= **88p**

Money problems

When you solve a word problem about money, draw the coins that you need.

Top tip!

Read the question carefully. If it is a subtraction problem, use partitioning or columns.

Example question: Tom has 48p and spends 15p. How much money does he have left?

You need to subtract 15p from 48p.

Method 1:
You could subtract the 10p and then the 5p (i.e. partition the 15p).

$$48p - 15p \quad = 48p - 10p - 5p$$
$$= 38p - 5p$$
$$= \textbf{33p}$$

Method 2:
Or you could use columns.

```
   T  U
   4  8  p
-  1  5  p
   3  3  p
```

Remember, start with the units.

Have a go!

> When you go shopping, think about which coins you need to buy something.
>
> What is the smallest number of coins you could use?

Test yourself

1. Which coins could you use to make 64p?
2. Max has 70p and spends 45p on an apple. How much money does he have left?

Time

The two hands of a clock show different parts of time.

minute hand

hour hand

The **shorter hand** is called the hour hand.
It is used to show the **hour**.

The numbers on the clock face are the hours.

The **longer hand** is called the minute hand. It is used to show **minutes**.

There are no numbers to help you read the minutes.

The minute hand takes 60 minutes to move all the way round the clock. There are 5 minutes between each number.

When the minute hand is:

- pointing at 12, it is o'clock
- quarter-way round, pointing at 3, it is quarter past
- half-way round, pointing at 6, it is half past
- three-quarters way round, pointing at 9, it is quarter to.

The hour hand is pointing at 2.

The minute hand is pointing at 12.

The time is 2 o'clock.

The hour hand is pointing past 2.

The minute hand is pointing at 3.

The time is quarter past 2.

The hour hand is pointing half-way between 2 and 3.

The minute hand is pointing at 6.

The time is half past 2.

The hour hand is pointing before 3.

The minute hand is pointing at 9.

The time is quarter to 3.

listen up
13

Keywords

Hour ➤ A unit of time; 1 hour is the same as 60 minutes

Minute ➤ A unit of time; 60 minutes make 1 hour

Parent tip!

Practise telling the time. Don't move on to 5 past and 10 past the hour, etc until your child understands quarter past, half past and quarter to.

Calculating time intervals

A **time interval** is how long it is between two different times.

To calculate a time interval, count forwards or backwards in minutes or hours, or both.

Remember, each time you move on a number, you have counted 5 minutes.

Example question 1: What is the time difference between these two clocks?

This clock says quarter past 6.

This clock says quarter to 7.

- Count forwards from quarter past 6 to quarter to 7 on the first clock face.
- Each time you move on a number, you have counted 5 minutes.

The answer is **30 minutes**.

Example question 2: What is the time difference between half past 3 and half past 4?

In this question there are no clocks, but you could imagine a clock.

Moving from half past one hour to half past the next hour means the hour hand has moved once round the clock face. This is 1 hour.

The answer is **1 hour**.

Sequencing time intervals

Events happen in time order.
You may need to put events in order.

Encourage your child to match quarter and half hours to the corresponding number of minutes.

 **Have a go!** Find out what time your favourite television programmes start.

Then find these times on a clock.

 **Test yourself**

1 What times are shown on these clocks?

a.  b.

2 How long is it between 4 o'clock and 6 o'clock?

3 How long is it between quarter to 12 and quarter past 12?

Measurement

This mind map will help you remember all the main points from this topic. Have a go at drawing your own mind map.

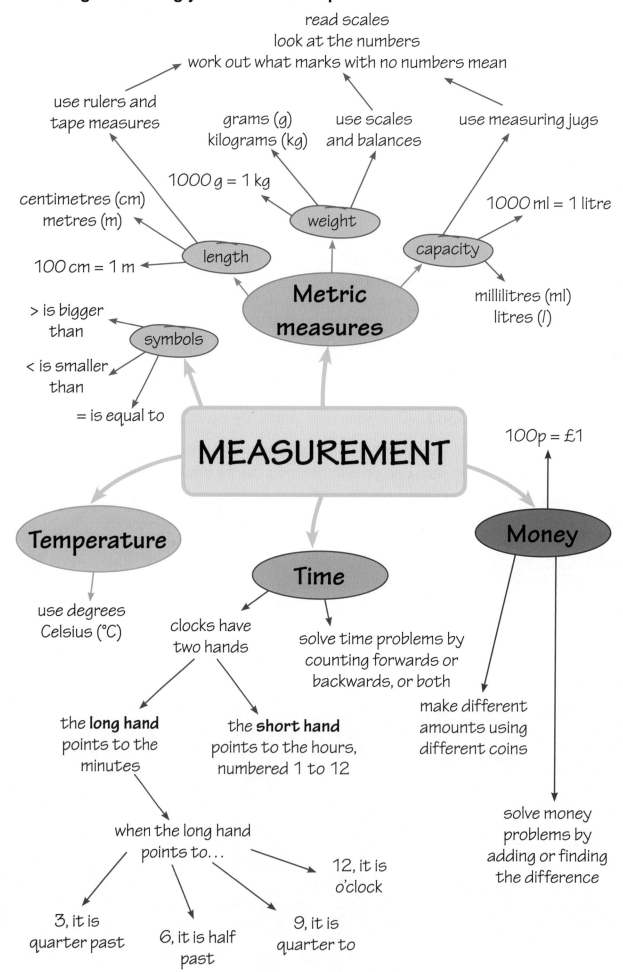

read scales
look at the numbers
work out what marks with no numbers mean

use rulers and
tape measures

grams (g)
kilograms (kg)

use scales
and balances

use measuring jugs

centimetres (cm)
metres (m)

1000 g = 1 kg

1000 ml = 1 litre

length

weight

capacity

100 cm = 1 m

> is bigger
than

symbols

**Metric
measures**

millilitres (ml)
litres (l)

< is smaller
than

= is equal to

MEASUREMENT

100p = £1

Temperature

Money

Time

use degrees
Celsius (°C)

clocks have
two hands

solve time problems by
counting forwards or
backwards, or both

make different
amounts using
different coins

the **long hand**
points to the
minutes

the **short hand**
points to the hours,
numbered 1 to 12

when the long hand
points to...

solve money
problems by
adding or finding
the difference

3, it is
quarter past

6, it is half
past

9, it is
quarter to

12, it is
o'clock

1 Write the missing numbers. **(3 marks)**

 a. 1 kg = ... g   **b.** 1 litre = ... ml   **c.** 1 m = ... cm

2 What is the length of the nail? **(1 mark)**

....

3 How much juice is in this jug?   **4** What is the weight of this parcel?

....

(1 mark)   **(1 mark)**

   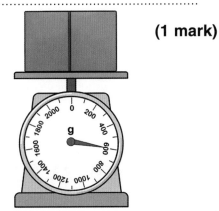

5 Write < or > in the circles below. **(3 marks)**

 a. 5 kg ◯ 7 kg   **b.** 500 g ◯ 250 g   **c.** 75 ml ◯ 80 ml

6 Which coins could you use to make 38p? **(1 mark)**

....

7 Ben uses two 20p coins to buy a pen for 28p. How much change
does he get? **(1 mark)**

....

8 What time is shown on each clock?

 a. **(1 mark)**   **b.** **(1 mark)**

 ....

9 How long is it from 2 o'clock to 6 o'clock? .... **(1 mark)**

10 How long is it from quarter past 7 to quarter past 8? .... **(1 mark)**

2D shapes

Here are some common **2D** shapes.
Shapes get their names from the number
of sides they have.

2D shapes have
the same number
of corners as the
number of their
sides.

Number of sides	Shape	Name	Sometimes shapes have sides that are all the same length
3		triangle	
4		quadrilateral	
5		pentagon	
6		hexagon	
8		octagon	

Quadrilaterals

There are different types of
quadrilateral.
Here are two examples.

square	rectangle
Squares have four equal sides.	Rectangles have two long sides that are equal and two short sides that are equal.
These two shapes have four **right angles**.	

Keywords

2D ➤ Two dimensional;
usually this means
having a length and a
width. 2D shapes are flat
and cannot be picked up
and handled

Rectangle ➤ A four-sided
shape that has four right
angles

Right angle ➤ A quarter
turn. Four quarter turns
make a full turn

Symmetry

This shape has symmetry.
If you fold the shape on the dotted line, the
two halves fit on top of one another exactly.

3D shapes

3D shapes have **faces**, **edges** and **vertices**.

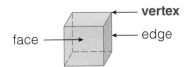

face

Here are some 3D shapes.

 cube
 cuboid
 prism
 pyramid

- 6 faces, each a square
- 8 equal edges
- 12 vertices

- 6 faces, each a rectangle
- 8 edges
- 12 vertices

- 2 end faces that are the same
- that shape runs through the whole shape

- a base
- the other faces are triangles that meet at one vertex

Some 3D shapes have curved surfaces.
- A **cone** has one face that is a circle.
- The other surface meets at one **apex**.

- A **cylinder** has two faces that are circles.
- The other surface is curved.

 cone

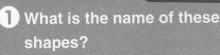 cylinder

Keywords

3D ➤ Three dimensional; usually this means having a length, width and height. 3D shapes can be picked up and handled

Face ➤ A side of a 3D shape

Edge ➤ A line where two faces meet

Vertices ➤ More than one vertex

Vertex ➤ A point or corner where two edges meet

Apex ➤ A point furthest from the base of a shape

Have a go!

Look for shapes at home and outside.

Use the proper name for the shapes.

Make sure you know the difference between 2D and 3D shapes.

Test yourself

1 What is the name of these shapes?
a.   b.

2 How many edges do these shapes have?
a.   b.

3 What shape are the faces of a cube?

Patterns and **sequences** can be made from numbers, shapes or objects.

Sequences

To find the next numbers in a sequence:

① look at the numbers in the sequence

② work out the sequence by subtracting the numbers or by counting forwards.

Example question: What are the next two numbers in this sequence?

3   5   7   9   11   13   __   __

+ 2   + 2   + 2   + 2   + 2

The sequence is to add 2, so keep adding 2.

So, 13 + 2 = **15** and 15 + 2 = **17**.

Remember, a sequence can use subtraction.

Example question: What is the next number in this sequence?

23   19   15   11   7   __

− 4   − 4   − 4   − 4   − 4

The sequence is to subtract 4, so keep subtracting 4.

The next number is 7 − 4 = **3**.

Sequences can have missing numbers.

Example question: What is the missing number in this pattern?

7   12   17   __   27   32   37

The pattern is to add 5.

+ 5   + 5   + 5   + 5   + 5   + 5   + 5

So, the missing number is 17 + 5 = **22**.

When you find number sequences, ask your child to try to work out the sequence and what comes next.

Parent tip!

Rules

If you are asked for the **rule** of a sequence, describe how you have worked out the sequence.

Example question: What is the rule for this sequence?

54   51   48   45   42   39

This is a subtracting sequence. Subtract 3 each time.

So the rule is **subtract 3** or **− 3**.

Listen up

15

Patterns

You can make patterns with shapes.

> **Example question:** What shape is next in this pattern?
>
>
>
> There are two triangles, then a circle, then two more triangles, then a circle.
>
> So, the next shape in the pattern is a **triangle**.

Keywords

Pattern ➤ Shapes or objects arranged to follow a rule
Sequence ➤ Numbers arranged to follow a rule
Rule ➤ Tells you how numbers or objects are arranged in a sequence or pattern

Patterns using colour

You might see patterns that use the same shapes but different colours.

> **Example question:** What colour should the next square in this pattern be?
>
>
>
> The pattern is a red square, two yellow squares and a green square.
> The third red square in the row is followed by a yellow square, so the next square will also be **yellow**.

 **Have a go!** Look for patterns around you. For example, on wallpaper, paving stones and fences.

Test yourself

1 What number comes next in this sequence?

17   27   37   47   57   ___

2 What shape comes next in this pattern?

 ___

3 What shape comes next in this pattern?

 ___

Rotating shapes

You can **rotate** (turn) a shape **clockwise** or **anti-clockwise**. Here are some quarter turns. A full turn takes the shape back to where it started.

clockwise turns			anti-clockwise turns		
$\frac{1}{4}$ turn	$\frac{2}{4}$ turn	$\frac{3}{4}$ turn	$\frac{1}{4}$ turn	$\frac{2}{4}$ turn	$\frac{3}{4}$ turn

When rotating a shape:

- check the turn you have been asked to make
- check the direction of the turn.

Example question: Rotate this shape $\frac{3}{4}$ anti-clockwise.

Check the turn you need to make

So, the shape will make three quarter turns, like this:

1st quarter turn

2nd quarter turn

3rd quarter turn $= \frac{3}{4}$ anti-clockwise turn

Trace or copy shapes.
Then let your child practise making different turns.

Parent tip!

Keywords

Rotate ➤ To turn a shape or object around a fixed point

Clockwise ➤ To turn in the same direction as the hands of a clock

Anti-clockwise ➤ To turn in the opposite direction as the hands of a clock

Listen up 16

Moving shapes

What to do:
1. Pick a vertex.
2. Move the vertex to where the question asks.
3. Mark the point.
4. Draw the shape in its new position.

Example question: Move shape A five squares to the right.

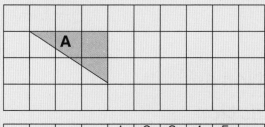

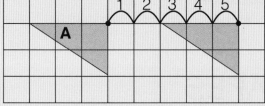

You may be asked to move a shape in two directions: left or right and up or down.
You might also have to say how a shape has moved.

What to do:
1. Pick a vertex.
2. Count the number of squares to the left or right.
3. Count the number of squares up or down.

Example question: How has rectangle 1 moved to rectangle 2?

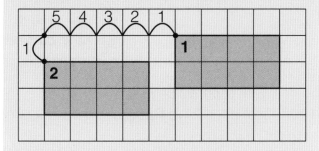

This rectangle has moved 5 squares left and 1 square down.

When moving a shape in a line, always keep it the same size. Do not rotate it.

Top tip!

Have a go!

Can you follow directions?
> Take two steps forwards.
> Turn right.
> Take three steps forwards.
> Turn left.
> Take five steps backwards.

Test yourself

1 Shape A is rotated and becomes Shape B.

What is the rotation?

2 How has square 1 moved to square 2?

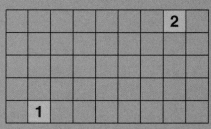

Geometry

This mind map will help you remember all the main points from this topic. Have a go at drawing your own mind map.

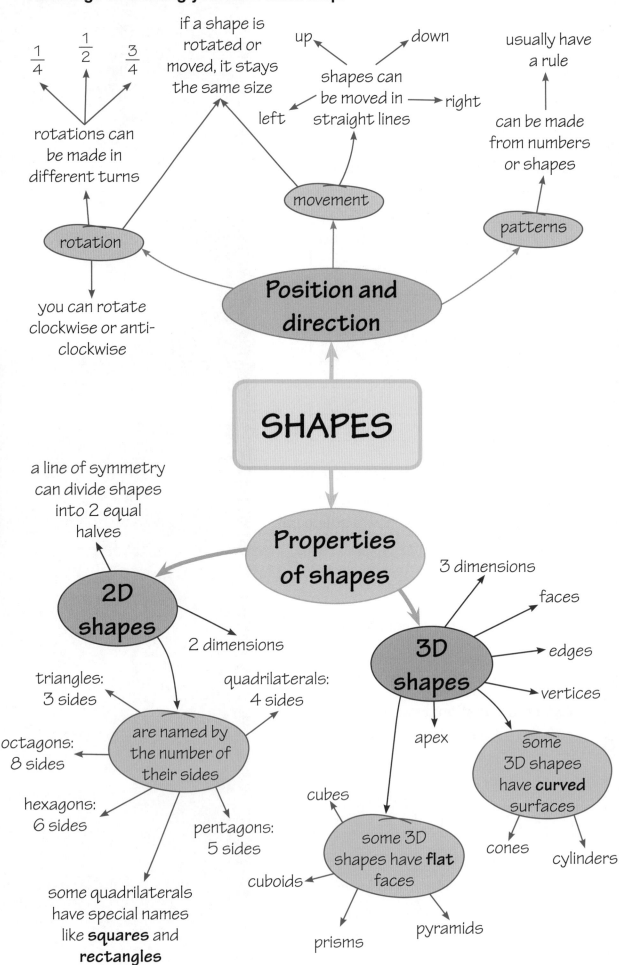

$\frac{1}{4}$ $\frac{1}{2}$ $\frac{3}{4}$

if a shape is rotated or moved, it stays the same size

up   down

shapes can be moved in straight lines

left   right

usually have a rule

can be made from numbers or shapes

rotations can be made in different turns

rotation

movement

patterns

you can rotate clockwise or anti-clockwise

Position and direction

SHAPES

a line of symmetry can divide shapes into 2 equal halves

Properties of shapes

2D shapes

2 dimensions

3D shapes

3 dimensions

faces

edges

vertices

apex

triangles: 3 sides

quadrilaterals: 4 sides

some 3D shapes have **curved** surfaces

octagons: 8 sides

are named by the number of their sides

hexagons: 6 sides

pentagons: 5 sides

cubes

cones   cylinders

some quadrilaterals have special names like **squares** and **rectangles**

cuboids

some 3D shapes have **flat** faces

prisms   pyramids

1 **a.** Why is this shape a triangle? **(2 marks)**

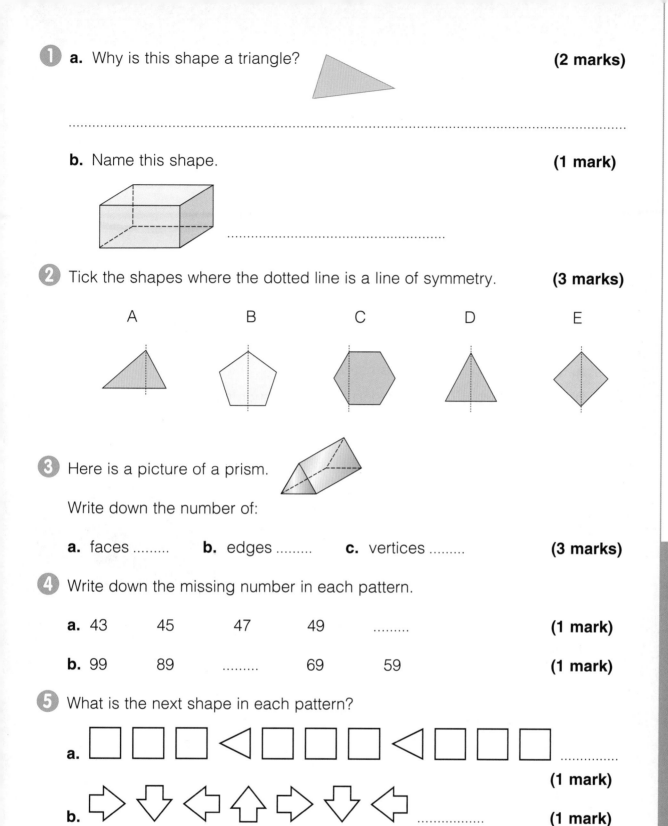

....

b. Name this shape. **(1 mark)**

....

2 Tick the shapes where the dotted line is a line of symmetry. **(3 marks)**

A   B   C   D   E

3 Here is a picture of a prism.

Write down the number of:

a. faces ....   **b.** edges ....   **c.** vertices ....   **(3 marks)**

4 Write down the missing number in each pattern.

a. 43   45   47   49   ....   **(1 mark)**

b. 99   89   69   59   **(1 mark)**

5 What is the next shape in each pattern?

a. .... **(1 mark)**

b. .... **(1 mark)**

6 A shape is rotated. What is the rotation shown by Shape 1 to Shape 2? **(1 mark)**

Shape 1   Shape 2

....

Bar charts

A **bar chart** shows information using bars or blocks.

A bar chart has:

- a **title** to tell you what the bar chart is about (the main title below is 'School lunches')
- a **scale** (on the scale below the numbers go up in twos).

Top tip! To read a scale, look at the numbers and work out what the spaces mean.

Example question: The bar chart shows what some children had for their school lunch.

a. How many children had a hot meal?

b. How many more children had a packed lunch than a sandwich?

School lunches

Number of children / Type of meal

a. ❶ Find the hot meal bar.

❷ Go to the top of the bar and follow the line to the number on the vertical axis.

14 children had a hot meal.

b. ❶ Work out how many children had a packed lunch and how many had a sandwich.

❷ Subtract the two numbers.

8 – 5 = **3 more children** had a packed lunch

Keywords

Bar chart ➤ A bar chart shows information as a picture. It uses bars or blocks on a graph

Scale ➤ The way the numbers are spread out on the axis of a graph (a line that is used to build a bar chart)

Pictogram ➤ A chart; uses pictures or symbols to stand for numbers

Listen up 17

Pictograms

A **pictogram** is like a bar chart that is made up of small pictures or symbols. It has:

- a **title** to tell you what the pictogram is about (the title below is 'School clubs')
- **one axis** (line) to tell you more information (the line below tells you the different clubs); you can also have pictograms with a horizontal line (axis)
- a **scale** to tell you the number shown by each symbol (the scale below means every smiley face is 2 children and half a smiley face is 1 child).

Example question: This pictogram shows the clubs attended by some children at a school.

How many children go to football club?

1. Find the row showing the football club.
2. Count the number of symbols.
3. Check the scale.
4. Work out the number. Here, there are four symbols and each symbol is worth 2 children, so 4 × 2 = 8.

8 children go to football club.

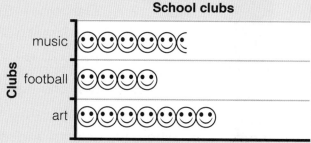

Pictogram symbols

You can use different symbols in a pictogram.

A symbol can stand for any number.

Try making your own pictogram.

- ➤ Choose a subject, e.g. pets or cars.
- ➤ Choose a symbol.
- ➤ Decide how many items will stand for each symbol.
- ➤ Work out how many symbols each group needs.
- ➤ Draw your pictogram.

Test yourself

1. Look at the 'School lunches' bar chart.

   a. How many children had a packed lunch?

   b. What was the least popular lunch?

2. Look at the 'School clubs' pictogram.

   a. How many more children were in the art club than the music club?

   b. How many different clubs are there?

Tables

Tables can show all kinds of information such as:

- class lists
- addresses
- multiplication facts.

Good tables show information clearly and are easy to read. They need titles so you know what they are about.

Example question 1:

How old is Bob?

Contact list for Class B

Name	Age	Address	Phone
Abi	7	6 Oakfield	5327802
Bob	6	3 Tay Street	5347723
Deb	7	9 Park Close	5326433

- Find Bob's **row** and the **column** showing 'Age'.
- Where the column and row meet, read the age.

Bob is **6**.

Example question 2:

What is 5×10?

A multiplication table

×	2	5	10
2	4	10	20
5	10	25	50
10	20	50	100

- Find the row for 5 and the column for 10.
- Where the row and column meet, read the answer.

The answer is **50**.

Example question 3:

What time and channel is the Art programme?

TV programmes

Time	Channels		
	BBC 1	CBBC	CBeebies
5 o'clock	Quiz	Blue Peter	Cartoon
Half past 5	Cooking	Cartoon	Puppets
6 o'clock	News	Art	Cartoon
Half past 6	Local news	Pets	Story

- Find Art in the lists of programmes.
- Go left on the row to find the time.
- Go up the column to find the channel.

Art is on **CBBC** at **6 o'clock**.

Top tip!

Read the title of the table to find out what it is about. Read the titles of the rows and columns, and use them to help you find information.

Keywords

Row ➤ The information that runs across a table (horizontal)

Column ➤ The information that runs up and down a table (vertical)

Tally charts

Tables can show information that has been counted. These are called **tally charts**.

It can be hard to remember what you have counted if you are counting different things at once.

To help, use a **tally**.

Each time you count forward, make a mark like a number one.

1 = | 2 = || 3 = ||| 4 = ||||

When you get to 5, draw a line through the four marks, like this: 5 = |||||

Then start the next 5. 6 = ||||| |

Count in fives and add on any extra ones for the total.

> **Example question:** What number is this tally?
>
> ||||| ||||| ||||| ||||| |||
>
> There are 4 groups of 5 plus 3 = **23**

You might see tallies written like this: ||||| |||||

They all work in the same way.

Top tip!

Using tally charts

Sam has counted the number of pets owned by children in his class. He has used a tally and put the information into a table.

Pet	Tally	Number
dog	||||| ||||| ||	12
cat	||||| ||||	9
rabbit	|||||	5
guinea pig	||	2
hamster	|||||	5
bird	||||	4

You might be asked questions about the table.

> **Example question:** How many more cats are there than birds?
>
> There are 9 cats and 4 birds.
>
> 9 – 4 = 5, so there are **5 more cats than birds**.

Keyword

Tally ➤ Recording what you count by making marks; you count in fives

Have a go!

Look for tables in newspapers and books. Also look at bus and train timetables, and TV listings.

➤ Work out what information they are telling you.

Test yourself

❶ Here is part of a table:

Name	Hair colour	Eye colour	Age
Ted	blond	blue	6
Mia	black	brown	7

a. What colour are Ted's eyes?

b. Who has black hair?

❷ What number is this tally?

||||| ||||| ||||| ||

❸ Write a tally for 21.

Statistics

This mind map will help you remember all the main points from this topic. Have a go at drawing your own mind map.

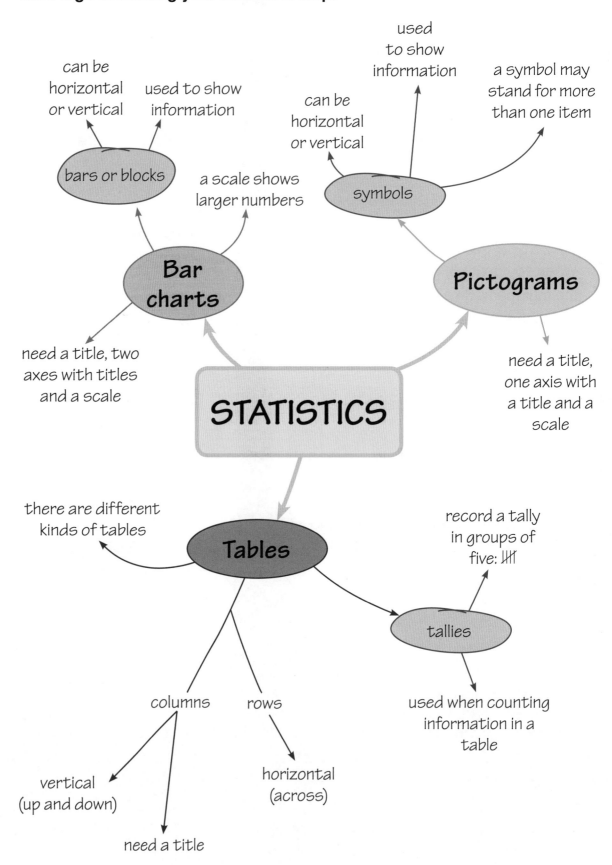

can be horizontal or vertical

used to show information

bars or blocks

a scale shows larger numbers

used to show information

can be horizontal or vertical

a symbol may stand for more than one item

symbols

Bar charts

Pictograms

need a title, two axes with titles and a scale

STATISTICS

need a title, one axis with a title and a scale

there are different kinds of tables

Tables

record a tally in groups of five: ⵏⵏⵏ

tallies

columns

rows

used when counting information in a table

vertical (up and down)

horizontal (across)

need a title

1 This bar chart shows some children's favourite school visits.

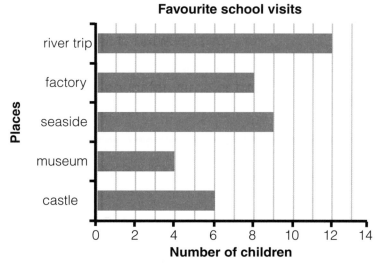

a. How many children enjoyed visiting the factory the most? **(1 mark)**

....

b. How many more children preferred the visit to the castle rather

than the museum? .... **(2 marks)**

2 This pictogram shows how many different flavours of ice cream were sold in an afternoon on a Devon beach.

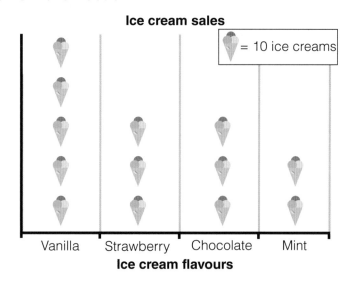

a. How many vanilla ice creams were sold? .... **(1 mark)**

b. Which two flavours had the same number of sales? **(2 marks)**

....

c. How many more strawberry ice creams were sold than mint
ice creams? **(2 marks)**

....

d. Which was the most popular flavour? **(2 marks)**

....

1 Write the next four numbers in each sequence.

    a. 5   7   9   11   ....   **(2 marks)**

    b. 3   13   23   33   ....   **(2 marks)**

2 Write the missing numbers.   **(2 marks)**

    a. 63 = ... tens and ...... units

    b. ...... = 2 tens and 6 units

3 Work out: **(4 marks)**

    a. 4 + 5 + 9 = ...

    b. 12 + 35 = ...

    c. 16 – 9 = ...

    d. 41 – 23 = ...

4 Write the missing numbers.   **(3 marks)**

    a. 24 – ...... = 17

    b. 28 + ... = 45

    c. 57 – ...... = 29

5 Work out the answers.   **(4 marks)**

    a. 6×2 = ...

    b. 4×10 = ...

    c. $30 \div 5$ = ...

    d. $70 \div 10$ = ...

6 Faith has 57 marbles. She loses 17 marbles. How many marbles does she have left?   **(2 marks)**

    ....

7 Kassim plants 48 seeds. Fay plants 34 seeds. How many seeds do they plant altogether?   **(2 marks)**

    ....

8 Harry has 40 stickers. He puts them all in a book, with 5 stickers on each page. How many pages does he use? **(2 marks)**

....

9 Alex plants 10 rows of 6 roses. How many roses does she plant? **(2 marks)**

....

10 Circle the odd numbers. **(3 marks)**

56   63   71   88   49   76

11 Circle the even numbers. **(3 marks)**

52   47   64   89   43   80

12 What fraction of this shape is shaded? **(1 mark)**

....

13 What fraction of these counters are white? **(1 mark)**

....

14 Work out: **(3 marks)**

a. $\frac{1}{2}$ of 14   **b.** $\frac{1}{3}$ of 12   **c.** $\frac{3}{4}$ of 20

....

15 Raj has 18 sweets. He gives half to his brother. How many sweets does he have left? **(2 marks)**

....

16 Ella has £20. She saves $\frac{1}{4}$ of the money and spends the rest. How much does she save? **(2 marks)**

....

17 Write the missing numbers. **(4 marks)**

a. 100 centimetres = ... metre   **b.** 2 litres = ... millilitres

c. 5 metres = ... centimetres   **d.** 2000 grams = ... kilograms

18 Write <, > or = in each circle. **(4 marks)**

a. 8 kg ◯ 3 kg

b. 5000 g ◯ 7000 g

c. 7 m ◯ 10 m

d. 2000 g ◯ 2000 g

19 **a.**

What time is it?

b.

What time is it? **(2 marks)**

....

20 How long is it from half past two to half past six? **(1 mark)**

....

21 How long is it from quarter to three to quarter to five? **(1 mark)**

....

22 Make 28p using the fewest number of coins. **(1 mark)**

....

23 Dee uses one 20p coin and two 5p coins to buy a bag of sweets for 27p. How much change does she get? **(2 marks)**

....

24 Draw a different set of coins that is worth the same as the coins below. **(1 mark)**

25 How can you tell that this is a pentagon? **(2 marks)**

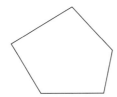

....

26 Name this shape. **(1 mark)**

....

27 Tick the shapes where the dotted line is a line of symmetry. **(2 marks)**

      A   B   C   D

28 This is a cuboid. Fill in the missing numbers. **(3 marks)**

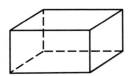

    a. A cuboid has .... faces.

    b. A cuboid has .... edges.

    c. A cuboid has .... vertices.

29 Write the missing number. **(1 mark)**

45   43   41   37   35   33

30 Draw the next shape in this pattern.   **(1 mark)**

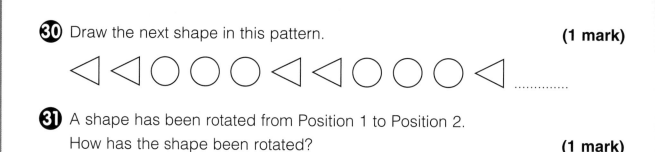

31 A shape has been rotated from Position 1 to Position 2.
How has the shape been rotated?   **(1 mark)**

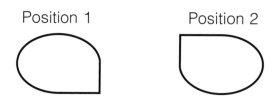

Position 1   Position 2

....

32 The rectangle moves from Position A to Position B.
Complete this sentence.   **(2 marks)**

The shape has moved .... squares to the ....

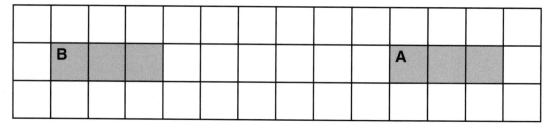

33 Some children collected money for charity.
This bar chart shows how much they collected.

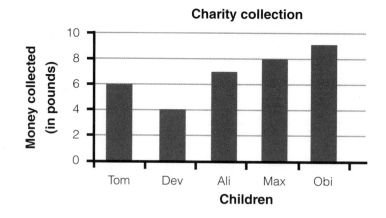

Look at the bar chart and then answer the questions on the next page.

a. Who collected the most money? **(1 mark)**

....

b. How much money did Max collect? **(1 mark)**

....

c. How much more money did Tom collect than Dev? **(1 mark)**

....

....

d. Who collected £7? **(1 mark)**

....

34 This table shows information about some animals.

Animal	Legs	Wings	Tail	Fur
Fox	4	0	Yes	Yes
Worm	0	0	No	No
Robin	2	2	Yes	No

a. How many legs does a worm have?

.... **(1 mark)**

b. Which animals have no fur?

.... **(2 marks)**

c. Which animal has no wings and fur?

.... **(2 marks)**

d. Does a robin have a tail?

.... **(1 mark)**

Answers

NUMBER AND PLACE VALUE

Test yourself questions

page 5 Counting forwards and back

1 **a.** 49 47 45 43
b. 60 63 66 69
c. 56 51 46 41
d. 51 61 71 81
e. 81 78 75 72

page 7 Place value

1 **a.** 67 = **60** + 7
b. **59** = 50 + 9
c. 28 = 20 + **8**

2 **a.** 63 + 20 = **83**
b. 87 – 5 = **82**
c. 68 – 40 = **28**

page 9 Numbers and number lines

1 **a.** 83
b. 68

2 50

page 11 More about numbers

1 **a.** 83 > 81
b. 91 > 57
c. 17 < 32
d. 77 > 68

2 81 56 30 27 24

3 72

Practice questions

page 13

1 **a.** 47 50 53 56 59 **(1 mark)**
b. 47 42 37 32 27 **(1 mark)**
c. 92 94 96 98 100 **(1 mark)**
d. 45 55 65 75 85 **(1 mark)**

2 **a.** 68 = **6** tens and **8** units **(1 mark)**
b. **78** = 7 tens and 8 units **(1 mark)**
c. 91 = **9** tens and **1** unit **(1 mark)**
d. **3**4 = 3 tens and **4** units **(1 mark)**

3 **a.** 37 **(1 mark)**
b. 62 **(1 mark)**

4 17 18 71 78 81 87
(**4 marks**: Award **2 marks** for six correct numbers or award **1 mark** for four or five correct numbers. Award **1 mark** for ordering the numbers and **1 mark** for starting with the lowest.)

5 **a.** 56 > 28 **(1 mark)**
b. 79 < 83 **(1 mark)**

6 fifty-nine **(1 mark)**

7 45 **(1 mark)**

CALCULATIONS

Test yourself questions

page 15 Adding and subtracting

1 **a.** 18
b. 45
c. 21
d. 106

2 **a.** 19
b. 2
c. 9
d. 55

page 17 Multiplying and dividing

1 **a.** 15
b. 8
c. 70
d. 35

2 **a.** 6
b. 8
c. 6
d. 9

3 **a.** ×
b. ÷

page 19 Problem solving

1 **a.** 56 + **27** = 83
b. 70 – **8** = 62
c. 4 + **8** + 3 = 15

2 Odd numbers: 15 93 81
Even numbers: 70 28 52 36

3 **a.** 4 × 3 = 12 or 3 × 4 = 12 or 12 ÷ 4 = 3 or 12 ÷ 3 = 4
b. 6 × 2 = 12 or 2 × 6 = 12 or 12 ÷ 6 = 2 or 12 ÷ 2 = 6

Practice questions

page 21

1 **a.** 11 **(1 mark)**
b. 3 **(1 mark)**
c. 8 **(1 mark)**
d. 6 **(1 mark)**

2 **a.** 13 **(1 mark)**
b. 19 **(1 mark)**
c. 18 **(1 mark)**
d. 17 **(1 mark)**

3 **a.** 74 **(1 mark)**
b. 78 **(1 mark)**
c. 54 **(1 mark)**

4 **a.** 34 + **9** = 43 **(1 mark)**
b. 5 × **10** = 50 **(1 mark)**
c. **10** ÷ 2 = 5 **(1 mark)**

5 34 56 ⑦ ㉙ 74 ⑲ 90
(**2 marks**: Award **1 mark** for 2 correct numbers and no incorrect numbers.)

6 a. ×   (**1 mark**)
   b. ÷   (**1 mark**)

7 a. 6 × 5 = 30
      (**2 marks**: Award **1 mark** for calculation 6 × 5 (accept 5 × 6) and **1 mark** for the answer 30.)
   b. 9 × 2 = 18
      (**2 marks**: Award **1 mark** for calculation 9 × 2 (accept 2 × 9) and **1 mark** for the answer 18.)

8 a. 70 cards
      (**2 marks**: Award only **1 mark** for correct method (e.g. 45 + 25 =) but the wrong answer.)
   b. 42 pages
      (**2 marks**: Award only **1 mark** for correct method (e.g. 70 − 28 =) but the wrong answer.)
   c. 4 seeds
      (**2 marks**: Award only **1 mark** for correct method (e.g. 20 ÷ 5 =) but the wrong answer.)

FRACTIONS

Test yourself questions
page 23 What are fractions?

1 a. $\frac{1}{3}$

   b. $\frac{1}{4}$

2 C

page 25 Finding fractions

1 2

2 a. 3
   b. 2
   c. 5

3 a. 6
   b. 9
   c. 15

Practice questions
page 27

1 a. $\frac{2}{4}$ (accept $\frac{1}{2}$)   (**1 mark**)

   b. $\frac{3}{4}$ (**1 mark**)

   c. $\frac{1}{4}$ (**1 mark**)

   d. $\frac{1}{3}$ (**1 mark**)

2 a. Any one of the three sections should be shaded.
                                                                                  (**1 mark**)
   b. Any three of the four sections should be shaded.
                                                                                  (**1 mark**)

3 a. 3   (**1 mark**)
   b. 5   (**1 mark**)
   c. 12   (**1 mark**)
   d. £20   (**1 mark**)

4 $\frac{9}{12}$ $\left(\text{accept } \frac{3}{4}\right)$ (**1 mark**)

5 a. 10 cards   (**1 mark**)
   b. 3 teddy bears   (**1 mark**)

6 B and C   (**2 marks**)

MEASUREMENT

Test yourself questions
page 29 Units and scales

1 70 g

2 8 cm

Page 31 Comparing measures

1 a. 6 m < 10 m
   b. 17 kg > 11 kg
   c. 75 cm < 80 cm

2 Child to tick statement b.
   (100 cm is twice 50 cm)

page 33 Money

1 Accept any correct answer, e.g. 50p, 10p, 2p, 2p

2 25p

page 35 Time

1 a. 8 o'clock
   b. Quarter to 5

2 2 hours

3 30 minutes or $\frac{1}{2}$ hour

Practice questions
page 37

1 a. 1000 g   (**1 mark**)
   b. 1000 ml   (**1 mark**)
   c. 100 cm   (**1 mark**)

2 8 cm   (**1 mark**)

3 4 litres   (**1 mark**)

4 600 g   (**1 mark**)

5 a. 5 kg < 7 kg   (**1 mark**)
   b. 500 g > 250 g   (**1 mark**)
   c. 75 ml < 80 ml   (**1 mark**)

6 Accept any set of coins that total 38p,
   e.g. 20p, 10p, 5p, 2p, 1p   (**1 mark**)

7 12p   (**1 mark**)

8 a. half past 10   (**1 mark**)
   b. quarter past 9   (**1 mark**)

9 4 hours   (**1 mark**)

10 1 hour (accept 60 minutes)   (**1 mark**)

GEOMETRY

Test yourself questions

page 39 Properties of shapes

1 a. triangle
   b. pentagon

2 a. 12
   b. 8

3 square

page 41 Patterns and sequences

1 67

2 a yellow square

3 a pink triangle

page 43 Position and direction

1 $\frac{1}{2}$ turn (clockwise or anti-clockwise)

2 6 squares right, 4 squares up

Practice questions

page 45

1 a. It has 3 sides. It has 3 corners.
       (**2 marks**: Award **1 mark** for each statement.)
   b. cuboid   (1 mark)

2 Child should tick B, D, E.
   (**3 marks**: Award **1 mark** for each answer.)

3 a. 5   (1 mark)
   b. 9   (1 mark)
   c. 6   (1 mark)

4 a. 51   (1 mark)
   b. 79   (1 mark)

5 a. triangle   (1 mark)
   b. arrow pointing upwards   (1 mark)

6 $\frac{1}{4}$ turn clockwise or $\frac{3}{4}$ turn anti-clockwise
                                                (1 mark)

STATISTICS

Test yourself questions

page 47 Charts and pictograms

1 a. 8 children
   b. sandwich

2 a. 3 children
   b. 3 clubs

page 49 Tables and tally charts

1 a. blue
   b. Mia

2 17

3 ⅢⅢ Ⅲ Ⅲ Ⅲ Ⅲ Ⅲ |

Practice questions

page 51

1 a. 8 children   (1 mark)
   b. 2 children   (2 marks)

2 a. 50 ice creams   (1 mark)
   b. strawberry and chocolate   (2 marks)
   c. 10 ice creams   (2 marks)
   d. vanilla   (2 marks)

MIXED PRACTICE QUESTIONS

pages 52–57

1 a. 13, 15, 17, 19   (2 marks)
   b. 43, 53, 63, 73   (2 marks)

2 a. 6 tens and 3 units   (1 mark)
   b. 26   (1 mark)

3 a. 18   (1 mark)
   b. 47   (1 mark)
   c. 7   (1 mark)
   d. 18   (1 mark)

4 a. 7   (1 mark)
   b. 17   (1 mark)
   c. 28   (1 mark)

5 a. 12   (1 mark)
   b. 40   (1 mark)
   c. 6   (1 mark)
   d. 7   (1 mark)

6 40 marbles
   (**2 marks**: Award **1 mark** for correct method (e.g. 57 – 17 =) and wrong answer.)

7 82 seeds
   (**2 marks**: Award **1 mark** for correct method (e.g. 48 + 34 =) and wrong answer.)

8 8 pages
   (**2 marks**: Award **1 mark** for correct method (e.g. 40 ÷ 5 =) and wrong answer.)

9 60 roses
   (**2 marks**: Award **1 mark** for correct method (e.g. 6 × 10 =) and wrong answer.)

10 56 ⑥③ ⑦① 88 ④⑨ 76 (**3 marks**: Award **1 mark** for each correct answer.)

11 ⑤② 47 ⑥④ 89 43 ⑧⓪ (**3 marks**: Award **1 mark** for each correct answer.)

12 $\frac{1}{4}$ (1 mark)

13 $\frac{2}{4}$ $\left(\text{accept } \frac{1}{2}\right)$ (1 mark)

14 a. 7   (1 mark)
    b. 4   (1 mark)
    c. 15   (1 mark)

15 9
(**2 marks**: Award **1 mark** for correct method (e.g. 18 ÷ 2 =) and wrong answer.)

16 £5 (**2 marks**: Award **1 mark** for correct method (e.g. 20 ÷ 4 =) and wrong answer.)

17 a. 1 metre (1 mark)
   b. 2000 millilitres (1 mark)
   c. 500 centimetres (1 mark)
   d. 2 kilograms (1 mark)

18 a. 8 kg > 3 kg (1 mark)
   b. 5000 g < 7000 g (1 mark)
   c. 7 m < 10 m (1 mark)
   d. 2000 g = 2000 g (1 mark)

19 a. 5 o'clock (1 mark)
   b. half past 7 (1 mark)

20 4 hours (1 mark)

21 2 hours (1 mark)

22 20p + 5p + 2p + 1p (1 mark)

23 3p
(**2 marks**: Award **1 mark** for correct totalling of coins to 30p. Award **1** further **mark** for correct method (e.g. 30 − 3 =) and wrong answer. Allow follow-through of incorrect total to an arithmetically correct answer for **1 mark**.)

24
 (1 mark)

There are different possible answers. They must total 56p.

25 It has 5 sides and 5 corners.
(**2 marks**: Award **1 mark** for each statement.)

26 pyramid (1 mark)

27 Child to tick shapes A and D.
(**2 marks**: Award **1 mark** for each correct answer.)

28 a. 6 (1 mark)
   b. 12 (1 mark)
   c. 8 (1 mark)

29 39 (1 mark)

30 ◁ (1 mark)

31 2 quarter turns or 1 half turn (1 mark)
(Accept with or without clockwise or anti-clockwise.)

32 The shape has moved **9** squares to the **left**.
(**2 marks**: Award **1 mark** for each correct answer.)

33 a. Obi (1 mark)
   b. £8 (1 mark)
   c. £2 (1 mark)
   d. Ali (1 mark)

34 a. 0 legs (1 mark)
   b. worm and robin (2 marks)
   c. fox (2 marks)
   d. yes (1 mark)

2D – Two dimensional; usually this means having a length and a width. 2D shapes are flat and cannot be picked up and handled

3D – Three dimensional; usually this means having a length, width and height. 3D shapes can be picked up and handled

Abacus – A tool for displaying numbers

Adding – Combining two or more numbers to give a total or a sum

Adding words – Words that show you may have to add, such as 'altogether', 'extra', 'more', 'plus', 'sum' and 'total'

Anti-clockwise – To turn in the opposite direction to the hands of a clock

Apex – A point furthest from the base of a shape

Bar chart – A bar chart shows information as a picture. It uses bars or blocks on a graph

Clockwise – To turn in the same direction as the hands of a clock

Column – The information that runs up and down a table (vertical)

Counting back – Counting numbers in reverse order, in a group (such as ones, twos, fives), so that the numbers get smaller

Counting forwards – Counting numbers in order, in a group (such as ones, twos, fives), so that the numbers get larger

Denominator – The bottom number in a fraction that shows the number of parts in the whole

Digit – A number from 0–9 that can be used to make other numbers

Dividing – To split or share a number equally

Division words – Words that show you may have to divide, such as 'each', 'every', 'half', 'quarter', 'share', 'split' and 'third'

Edge – A line where two faces meet

Even number – A number that can be divided exactly by 2

Face – A side of a 3D shape

Fraction – A number that shows the part or parts of one whole

Hour – A unit of time; 1 hour is the same as 60 minutes

Metric units – Measures based on groups of ten

Minute – A unit of time; 60 minutes make 1 hour

Multiplication words – Words that show you may have to multiply, such as 'by', 'double', 'lots', 'times' and 'twice'

Multiplying – Counting or adding in steps of the same number

Number line – Shows the position of a number. The numbers can be listed in different ways, for example ones, twos, fives, tens, and so on

Numerator – The top number in a fraction that shows the number of parts you have

Odd number – A number that cannot be divided exactly by 2

Partitioning – Splitting numbers using place value

Pattern – Shapes or objects arranged to follow a rule

Pence/pennies – A unit of money. 100 pennies make £1

Pictogram – A chart; uses pictures or symbols to stand for numbers

Place value – What a digit is worth. This depends on its position in a number

Pounds – A unit of money. 100 pence make £1. £1 is the same as 100 pennies

Rectangle – A four-sided shape that has four right angles

Right angle – A quarter turn. Four quarter turns make a full turn

Rotate – To turn a shape or object around a fixed point

Row – The information that runs across a table (horizontal)

Rule – Tells you how numbers or objects are arranged in a sequence or pattern

Scale – The way the numbers are spread out on the axis of a graph (a line that is used to build a bar chart)

Sequence – Numbers arranged to follow a rule

Subtracting – Taking one number from another to leave a difference

Subtracting words – Words that show you may have to subtract, such as 'difference', 'fewer', 'left', 'less than', 'minus', 'reduce' and 'take away'

Symbols – Signs that are used instead of words

Tally – Recording what you count by making marks; you count in fives

Vertex – A point or corner where two edges meet

Vertices – More than one vertex

Index